PRAYING

— A —

NEW STORY

Michael Morwood

ORBIS BOOKS

Maryknoll, New York 10545

Founded in 1970, Orbis Books endeavors to publish works that enlighten the mind, nourish the spirit, and challenge the conscience. The publishing arm of the Maryknoll Fathers and Brothers, Orbis seeks to explore the global dimensions of the Christian faith and mission, to invite dialogue with diverse cultures and religious traditions, and to serve the cause of reconciliation and peace. The books published reflect the views of their authors and do not represent the official position of the Maryknoll Society. To learn more about Maryknoll and Orbis Books, please visit our website at www.maryknoll.org.

Copyright © 2004 by Michael Morwood

Published by Orbis Books, Maryknoll, New York 10545-0308.

All rights reserved. No part of this publication may be reproduced or transmitted in any form or by any means, electronic or mechanical, including photocopying, recording, or any information storage or retrieval system, without prior permission in writing from the publisher.

Queries regarding rights and permissions should be addressed to: Orbis Books, P.O. Box 308, Maryknoll, NY 10545-0308.

Manufactured in the United States of America

Library of Congress Cataloging-in-Publication Data

Morwood, Michael.
    Praying a new story / Michael Morwood.
      p. cm.
    ISBN 1-57075-531-0 (pbk.)
    1. Catholic Church – Prayer-books and devotions – English.
  I. Title.
  BX2149.2 .M67 2004
  242'.802 – dc22

                                                  2003019885

Contents

John E. Argauer

There is a new story emerging in consciousness, one that evokes awe, wonder, and reverence as it expands our notion of God.

Introduction

It makes a big difference how we pray if we view God as a person in heaven or, as the Baltimore Catechism put it, if we view God "everywhere." For many of us prayer has been an effort to contact an "elsewhere God." What happens when we shift our attention to an "everywhere God" — a sustaining Presence in all, through all, never absent, never distant, not in one place more than in any other place, a Presence "in whom we live and move and have our being"?

This little book of prayers is an invitation to find out.

There is a new story emerging in consciousness, one that evokes awe, wonder, and reverence as it expands our notion of God. We are beginning to understand that God is not a person limited to a place and only vaguely present in the universe. We are beginning to appreciate a God alive in every particle in the billions of galaxies beyond us and in the grass or pavement beneath our feet. God is here, everywhere, and with us always.

When we expand our ideas and images of God, our beliefs and prayer life also deepen. A fresh understanding of Jesus emerges. Jesus still reveals our connectedness with God and reveals wonderful, freeing insights about human existence and its possibilities. But the salvation story comes to life in a broader context — in a universe immersed in God's presence, a Presence at work in all places, at all times, and in every human being who ever existed. In this new story, freed from images and notions of distance and separation, prayer is no longer concerned with addressing an elsewhere God.

Not surprisingly, many Christians whose faith has been enriched by the wonder of the new story now experience a genuine dilemma. They want to continue their practice of prayer but often find official formulas of prayer and even the patterns of their own private prayer unsuitable. They ask, "How do we pray now?" They may also wonder: "How does God *hear* our prayers?" or "Is prayer for God's sake or our sake?" These Christians are not calling prayer into question. They are simply seeking to incorporate the story of God ever present in an unfolding universe into their personal prayer life.

Traditional Christian teaching holds that prayer is concerned with raising the mind and heart to God. This remains true for us today. The purpose of this book is to help raise our minds and hearts to the God always present to us rather than address prayers to an elsewhere God. Beautiful examples of this type of prayer are found in the book of Psalms. Most of the psalms address God directly, but some are more meditative, inviting readers to reflect on the nature of God (see

Ps. 103, God Is Love) or on God's presence throughout history (see Ps. 105 or Ps. 78). These psalms
seek to build trust in God through remembrance and
reflection.

This pattern of prayer can be readily adapted to
help us incorporate a growing understanding of God's
presence in the world into our prayer life. The adapta-
tion will lead us into reflection on God always present
and everywhere active in an unfolding universe. It will
lead us to reflect on ourselves as a life-form giving
this Presence a wonderful way of coming to expression. It will lead us to reflect on Jesus, whose insights
about our connectedness with God withstand dramatic
changes in worldview. It will lead us to reflect on Christmas, Good Friday, Easter and Pentecost, intimacy,
suffering, sin and death in the belief that we live in God.

The prayers in *Praying a New Story* invite you into
this reflection. You can use the prayers for private, personal use in the same way you pray Psalm 105. Even
the prayers that have a distinctly "eucharistic" pattern
can be prayed this way as they invite you to reflect on
living and moving and being *in* God.

The eucharistic pattern of some of the prayers re-
flects the reality that this is the most familiar example
of Christian prayer incorporating the elements of remembrance and presence. However, a feature of traditional eucharistic prayer is the repetitive use of words
and images based on the fall-redemption story. The
challenge here is to shape other prayers with words

and imagery that resonate with an evolving under-standing of our ongoing relationship with God. This is not an easy task since the words we use will not have the familiarity of prayers we are accustomed to. But we have to make a start. It will take some time for us to find the best, most evocative ways to express our enriched beliefs about living in God and about our relationship with Jesus as we pray in the context of the new story. We will have to experiment with ideas and images, words and phrases, to find what works well and what does not. These prayers are offered as part of that experimentation. This creative endeavor is challenging and exciting and one in which we can all participate.

We can gather around the familiar and powerful symbols of bread and wine and use them to express a new story of our life in God with Jesus. We can allow that story to affirm us as bearers of the sacred as we eat and drink and commit ourselves to give witness to God's Spirit in our lives. These prayers do not require an ordained priesthood. That is reserved for the offi-cial public arena of worship. Here we simply want to find words and images that resonate with and nurture our journey in faith development and to allow familiar symbols, bread and wine, to touch our lives here and now in whatever way they can.

This book is not a manual on how to pray, nor is it a substitute for other books of prayer. While there are many ways to raise our minds and hearts to God, the prayers here simply focus on the new story and how we might pray within this context. The story itself unfolds throughout the prayers and reflections. It is a story of all life existing in God, of God's creative Spirit always and everywhere active as the universe itself bursts forth and as life develops on this planet. It is a story telling us that we ourselves give the mystery we call God a way of coming to expression. In this story God is never absent, never distant. Life is not a journey *to* God; it is a journey *in* God.

If the ultimate aim of prayer is to deepen our faith and nurture a healthy Christian spirituality, the test of this prayer, as with all prayer, will not be how intense and uplifting it was or what insights we had. It will be the extent to which it leads us to allow the Spirit of graciousness and generosity to be evident in the way we are neighbors to one another.

Finally, in response to the question, "How do we pray now?" I suggest in these pages that we do less talking *to* God, that we allow personal and group prayer to be more reflective about what it means to live *in* God and to allow God's presence to come to freer expression in us. While doing less talking to God may be a significant change in our pattern of prayer and may seem awkward at first, the reflective nature of our prayer can draw us into a deeper awareness of the richness of our Christian faith and the inspiring vision of life it offers.

A New Story to Tell

God Always and Everywhere

> We need a story that will educate us, a story that will heal,
> guide, and discipline us. —Thomas Berry*

Throughout history human beings have used the prevailing worldview to shape their beliefs and customs. The stories people tell about the beginning of the universe and the beginning of human life are fundamental to religious belief because these stories tell believers how they are in relationship with the spirit world or with their God. These stories tell people who they are and why they are the way they are. The stories give identity to religious communities and meaning to life.

We, too, look to the prevailing worldview. We recognize that here and now our statements of religious faith must be compatible with today's worldview; otherwise those statements will be irrelevant for people. We also want to affirm the wisdom contained in earlier stories shaped in a worldview quite different from

---

*Thomas Berry, *The Dream of the Earth* (San Francisco: Sierra Club Books, 1990), 124.

Mimi Forsyth

We must take into account all of creation and all human beings when we speak of God being present and active.

ours. We want to ensure those insights continue to be heard.

Today our worldview is very much shaped by scientific data about our universe and the development of life on earth. This "New Story," unknown to our ancestors, challenges all religious people to think in a religiously inclusive way. We *must* take into account all of creation and all human beings when we speak of God being present and active. Such an inclusive understanding has the capacity to heal, educate, and transform the human community.

Let us pray a new story about God, present and active in our world.

✠

We believe in God,
Source and Ground of all that exists.

We believe in God
present and active
from the beginning of time,
present to this time
and to time unfolding beyond our imagining.

We believe in God
present and active
everywhere
in a universe
with space and matter
beyond our imagination.

We believe in God
present and active
in hydrogen clouds
collapsing
to form billions of galaxies.

We believe in God
present and active
four billion years ago
when gas, ice, and rock came together

Megan McKenna

We believe in God present and active on this planet for billions of years before human life emerged.

to form planet earth
orbiting one of billions of stars
in the Milky Way galaxy.

We believe in God
present and active
on this planet
for billions of years
before human life emerged:
in the new beginnings,
in the upheavals,
in death and destruction,

and in the constant transformations
into new life and new possibilities.

We believe in God
present and active,
coming to visible expression
in a wonderful life-form
capable of making God's "reign" visible
here on earth
as nowhere else in the breadth of the universe.

We believe in God
present and active
everywhere on earth
in the slow development
of human cultures and societies,
in the growth of knowledge,
and in the constant search for meaning
as men and women
tell stories to explain their connectedness
with the mystery,
the Source and Sustainer of all that exists.

We believe in God
present and active
in Jesus of Nazareth,
revealing to us the good news
of our connectedness with God
and with all other people
and urging us to love

graciously and generously
so that God's reign might be established.

We believe in God
present and active
in our times,
prompting us who are Christian
to be more expansive and more inclusive
as we reflect on
our understanding of "God,"
the story of Jesus,
our connectedness with all people,
and our responsibility to make God's reign visible
through gracious generosity.

We take these gifts of the earth
and work of human hands,
bread and wine,
and we give thanks
for who we are
and all we have.
We break and share this bread,
as Jesus broke and shared it,
mindful of
God's presence with us
and our bonding with
all people.

We share this bread,
committing ourselves

to allow the mind and spirit of Jesus
to be evident in our living and loving.
May people see in us
the breadth of vision and compassion
we have seen in Jesus.

We take this wine,
mindful of the privilege
of human existence
and our ability
to appreciate our connectedness
with God, the Source of all that exists.

May people see in us
the spirit of appreciation, gratitude,
and generous self-giving
we have seen in Jesus.

Pause for quiet reflection.

May the story we tell
about God,
about our universe,
about all people,
and about ourselves
"educate,
heal,
guide,
and discipline us."

Our Dignity

A Story for All Human Beings

Together with everything that has ever existed in this universe, we exist *in* God. God is never absent. God is everywhere, involved in the unfolding of matter and life wherever this happens.

God, the Cause, Ground, Sustainer of all that exists, always has been and continues to be actively involved in the slow development of human life from the dust of stars. All human beings share the same origin. We share the dignity of participating in the mystery we call God.

✠

We give thanks
for the unfolding of
matter,
mind,
intelligence,
and life
that has brought us
to this moment in time.

We celebrate
our common origin
with everything that exists
and we celebrate
the mystery we call "God,"
the Ground and Sustainer
of everything that exists,
in whom we live and move and have our being.

We acknowledge
this awesome mystery
embodied
in every human person,
aware that
each gives God
unique and personal expression.

Here,
now,
God is everywhere present,
visible in every human person
who loves.

Here,
now,
God comes to visible expression
in each of us.

We give thanks for men and women
throughout human history
who sought to name

Katie Odell

We acknowledge this awesome mystery embodied in every human person, aware that each gives God unique and personal expression.

and articulate
our connectedness with all people,
with all of creation,
and with God.

We give thanks especially for Jesus of Nazareth.
He inspires us to name ourselves
as "temples of God's Spirit."
We rejoice in this freeing, good news,
and we seek to give this Spirit
generous expression in our lives.

Jesus challenges us
to look into our hearts,
to examine the way we are neighbor,
to overcome our prejudices,
to put an end to divisions,
to stretch our generosity,
to overcome our fear of the mystery,
to see God present in our everyday loving,
and to make the "reign" of love visible
throughout our world.

Through Jesus
we believe we are all
"sons and daughters"
of the one God.
We believe
the same Spirit of God
that came to visibility in Jesus
yearns for visible expression in us.

This is our common dignity
whatever our race or creed,
whatever our place or time.

We long to see our common dignity
proclaimed
and celebrated by all religions.
We pray that the one Spirit all people share
may be given free and generous expression
for the betterment of humanity
and our world. Amen.

God-with-Us

Temples of God's Spirit

When did human beings become "temples of God's Spirit"? Are we to believe this happened only after the death of Jesus? Or can we believe that human beings have always been temples of God's Spirit? Can we believe that God's Spirit has always been present in the slow development of the human species from its earliest beginnings? Can we believe that God's Spirit has been present in every human being who has ever walked this planet? Can we believe that we human beings give God a wonderful way of coming to expression?

Yes, we can. That is the good news. And our prayer seeks to deepen our belief.

✜

In the star we call the "sun," converting six hundred million tons of hydrogen into helium every second and doing so for more than four billion years:

We see the presence of the God in whom we believe.

24

Mimi Forsyth

In the star we call the "sun," we see the presence of God.

In all the other billions of stars in the Milky Way galaxy
and in all their planets:
We see the presence of the God in whom we believe.

In the hundreds of billions of other galaxies, each with
billions of stars:
We see the presence of the God in whom we believe.

In a universe beyond our comprehension, expanding a
billion miles every hour:
We see the presence of the God in whom we believe.

In a planet like Venus, barren and unable to support
life as we experience it on earth:
We see the presence of the God in whom we believe.

Here on earth where conditions are ideal for life to ap-
pear and prosper:
We see the presence of the God in whom we believe.

In the mysterious subatomic world:
We see the presence of the God in whom we believe.

In DNA, the building blocks of life:
We see the presence of the God in whom we believe.

In the development of life on earth for hundreds of millions of years:
We see the presence of the God in whom we believe.

In the upheavals on this planet that saw widespread destruction of life and new beginnings, long, long before human life emerged:
We see the presence of the God in whom we believe.

In the emergence of human life:
We see the presence of the God in whom we believe.

In the development of language:
We see the presence of the God in whom we believe.

In the use of tools:
We see the presence of the God in whom we believe.

In the development of writing and art:
We see the presence of the God in whom we believe.

In the growth of many and varied cultures:
We see the presence of the God in whom we believe.

In humankind's search for meaning:
We see the presence of the God in whom we believe.

In the great religious leaders:
We see the presence of the God in whom we believe.

In Jesus of Nazareth:
We see the presence of the God in whom we believe.

In you and in me:
We see the presence of the God in whom we believe.

✜

Do you realize that you are God's temple and that the
Spirit of God is living in you? (1 Cor. 3:16)

Your bodies are temples of the Holy Spirit.
(1 Cor. 6:19)

We are earthenware jars that hold this treasure, to
make it clear that such an overwhelming power comes
from God and not from us. (2 Cor. 4:7)

✠

We give expression
to the Spirit within us
and give thanks
for the wonder of who we are
and for our conscious awareness
of that Spirit
at work in everything that exists.

We give thanks
for Jesus
in whom that Spirit
was able to work freely
and was able to articulate
insights and convictions
that open our minds
to the presence
of the Spirit of Life
in our midst.

We give thanks,
as Jesus gave thanks,
using bread
to speak to us of earthen vessels
holding a treasure.

We break and share bread,
as Jesus broke and shared bread,
committing ourselves
to love generously
as "temples of God's Spirit."

We pledge ourselves to be
the "body of Christ"
loving God and neighbor
with all our hearts,
with all our minds,
and in all our actions.

We drink wine
as Jesus shared wine with his friends,
mindful of our bonding
with all that exists
through the Spirit
creatively present with and within us.

*Pause for quiet reflection on being
"a temple of God's Spirit."*

We see the presence of God in whom we believe
here now in us.

Eric Wheater

"A temple of God's Spirit."

We acknowledge
now to be our Pentecost time,
when God-with-us
seeks expression
in our actions
and in new words and images.

To being the presence of God in our world:
Amen. Amen.

Extravagant Generosity

Let Celebration Begin!

Jesus believed and taught that extravagant generosity is a key characteristic of God and of the "kingdom of God." His teaching urges us to recognize the connectedness between God's presence and being generous. When we see or experience generosity, we are to know that the Spirit of God is present and active here! We give the God of extravagant generosity a way of coming to expression.

Jesus often looked to nature to illustrate his teaching. A grain of wheat is "generous" in its dying because its death produces new life. If he were alive today, Jesus would doubtless look to the New Story of the universe to underscore his message.

In this passage from *The Universe Is a Green Dragon,* Brian Swimme conveys Jesus' insight with an image from the New Story. Like listeners two thousand years ago we are invited to hear, to ponder, and to pray about what we hear so that it may transform and expand our understanding of who we are.

Self-expression is the primary sacrament of the universe. Whatever you deeply feel demands to be given form and released. Profound joy insists upon song and dance. Don't ask anyone what to celebrate; don't even ask yourself! Let celebration begin. Let generosity of being happen. Nothing more is required.

Take supernovas as your models. When they had filled themselves with riches, they exploded in a vast cosmic celebration of their work. What would you have done? Would you have had the courage to flood the universe with your riches? Or would you have talked yourself out of it by pleading that you were too shy? Or hoarded your riches by insisting they were yours and that others did not deserve them because they did not work for them? Remember the supernova's extravagant generosity and celebration of being. It reminds us of our destiny as celebration become self-aware. We are Generosity-of-Being evolved into human form.*

✠

Let us pray:

We give thanks
for the Driving Force

---

*Brian Swimme, *The Universe Is a Green Dragon* (Santa Fe, N.Mex.: Bear & Company, 1984), 147.

at work in our universe
that becomes visible
in extravagant generosity
and celebration of being.

We give thanks
for our awareness
of this Driving Force at work,
mindful that it is beyond
the names we give to it,
beyond the images we use to describe it:

Source and Ground of all Being.
Supreme Spirit.
Allah.
Yahweh.
Creator.
Supreme Being.

Whatever names we use,
we acknowledge
that everything in existence
gives expression
to this Reality
we call "God."
We are able to rejoice in a universe
abounding in extravagant generosity
where disintegration and death
lead to new possibilities
of self-expression.

We rejoice
that here on earth
we are a life-form where
Life,
Love,
Intelligence,
and Awareness
come to expression in human form.

We rejoice
and want to celebrate
that we are "Generosity-of-Being
evolved into human form."

We give thanks
for the wonder of human existence
that enables Generosity-of-Being
to speak and sing,
laugh and dance,
write and paint,
plan and build,
imagine possibilities,
appreciate,
celebrate,
and rejoice.

We celebrate the men and women
throughout human history
who have lived life fully
and in their extravagant generosity

have led us to move beyond ideas and images and
    behavior
that locked us into fear,
timidity, selfishness,
and a diminished understanding
of our true selves.

We give thanks especially
for Jesus of Nazareth,
who so allowed the Spirit of extravagant generosity
to move in his life
that we recognize in him
the wonder of the Spirit in human form,
and have come to see in him
the truth that we are all
"Generosity-of-Being evolved into human form."

Mindful, as Jesus was,
of what is hidden to our eyes,
we take bread, remembering a Power,
a Presence
we cannot see
but believing this Presence
carries and supports us always
in ordinary, everyday living.

We break this bread

~ a star explodes and gives its all for new possibilities

~ a grain of wheat dies that we may be fed

~ *Generosity-of-Being in what seems so ordinary*
~ *Jesus who gave all he had for Love's sake*
~ *Bread, you and I — blessed, broken, and given*
~ *Bread, you and I — and a Presence we cannot see but in which we believe*
~ *You and I — called to be "Generosity-of-Being evolved into human form"*

and share it.

We drink,
as Jesus drank with his friends,
mindful of our bonding with Generous Love,
and commit ourselves
to allow Generous Love
free rein in our lives.

Time for quiet reflection: I am Generosity-of-Being evolved into human form.

We say "Yes" to *being* the body of Christ.
We say "Yes" to *being* Generosity-of-Being in human form.
We say "Yes" to each of us holding a treasure.
We say "Yes" to loving generously.

(What is my particular "Yes" for this day?
For this time of my life?)

Understanding Prayer

The Breath of Life in Us

Christians who have believed that prayer is concerned with contacting an elsewhere God now face a radical shift in their understanding of prayer. Prayer is not so much about talking to or addressing God, but rather about deepening our awareness that God — the Breath of Life present throughout the universe — comes to visible expression in us. When we reflect on this truth, we deepen our wonder and joy about who we are, we appreciate the story of Jesus more than ever before, and we understand better what it means to say "Yes" to being the "Body of Christ."

✠

We gather to pray,
believing that
God,
Source, Empowerer,
Breath, Enlivener,
and Energizer
prays in us.

We pray,
aware that
God at work
in the vastness of this universe
for billions of years
comes to visible
and audible expression
in our words
of appreciation.

We rejoice
in the Breath
breathing life and vitality
into our world,
into our lives
and into our gathering here,
connecting us
at the deepest level
with all that exists.

We rejoice
in the wonder of who we are,
bearers of the Breath of Life,
privileged
in our awareness of this,
and challenged
by our privilege
to allow the Breath of Life
full expression
in our living and loving.

We call to mind
Jesus of Nazareth,
who opened minds and hearts
to this awareness
and to this challenge.
The Breath of Life
moved so freely and openly
in his life
that people recognized
the relationship
at the deepest level of being
between God and a human person.

In Jesus
we have come to see
the truth of who we are
and we give thanks for his life,
his teaching,
and the courage with which
he faced death
and the mystery
of relationship
with the Breath of Life
beyond death.

We take this bread,
as Jesus took bread,
mindful of the Breath of Life,
always present,
always sustaining,

always nourishing,
and we give thanks
for that Breath
and the wonder of who we are.

We break this bread
recalling Jesus' readiness
to love
with all his heart,
with all his soul,
with all his strength,
with all his mind,
and to love his neighbor
as he loved himself.

We eat this bread,
praying that the generosity
of the Breath of Life
may find free expression
in our lives.

We take this wine,
mindful of the Breath of Life
bonding us with all that exists
in its fecundity
diversity,
complexity,
and supporting systems.

We drink
with appreciation,

with respect,
and with gratitude
for that bonding.

Time for silent reflection:
The Breath of Life prays in me.

May we allow the Breath of Life
to be evident in our words and actions,
in our homes,
in our workplaces,
in all our relationships,
and in our world.
Amen.

Prayer for the New Story

Expressing Who We Are

As we embrace the New Story we should become more familiar with a prayer form that deepens our awareness of who we are — a life-form giving the Creator Spirit a unique way of coming to expression. Jesus mirrors this reality for us and to us.

This prayer form does not address God or ask God to intervene and change the way things are. Rather it leads us to reflect on the wonder of God coming to expression in and among us. This is the Wow! of human existence from a Christian perspective. It is also the responsibility we each carry.

✜

We pray,
conscious that
raising our hearts and minds
is a gift of the Spirit of Life
at work
in the depths of our being.
For the presence of that Spirit in us, we give thanks.

Eric Wheater

We are bearers of a treasure, the Spirit of Life blessing us with a variety of gifts.

We pray,
conscious that
our prayer
gives the Spirit
a way of breaking into word and song
unique in all the universe.
For the words and songs within each of us, we give
thanks.

We pray,
believing
we are bearers of a treasure,
the Spirit of Life
blessing us with a variety of gifts.
For the treasures we each bear, we give thanks.

We pray,
mindful of men and women
throughout human history
who allowed the Spirit of Life
to work in them
for the betterment
of our world and humanity.
For their lives and their inspiration, we give thanks.

We pray,
remembering Jesus
who so allowed the Spirit of Life
to move in his life
that in him we have seen
the perfect expression
of the Spirit in human form.
For Jesus and all he means to us, we give thanks.

We pray,
challenged by Jesus
to allow his life
to be a mirror for us
so that we might live life in all its fullness.

We pray,
mindful
of all that has brought us together,
of the Spirit at work in our lives
and of what may be possible
if we allow the Spirit
to work freely in each of us.

We pray,
inviting
the Spirit of Life, Love, and Goodness
to move freely in our words and actions.

Silent reflection.

One Body

Bonded with the Universe

We believe that God is the Ground of everything that exists, that everything exists *in* God. Everything and everyone we see in this universe participates in God, and gives God a way of coming to expression.

We are products of God's creative presence in our universe for billions and billions of years. God's presence anywhere in the universe operates in and through what is there to be worked with. Earth is quite different from Venus, yet the same Presence is operative in each planet.

So too with us. God works in and through what God has to work with: changing worldviews, different cultures, personalities, individual giftedness, institutionalized religion, our developing knowledge about the universe and our planet, and human limitations. We are all connected *in* God and we give God wonderfully diverse ways of coming to visibility.

✠

We are all part of one body
and we pray as sharers of one body
delighting in our capacity
to appreciate diversity in unity.

We are one with the billions of galaxies
and one with their billions of stars.
Their living and their dying
make our existence possible.
In us, the atoms they create
produce a life-form
with the wonderful gifts of awareness
and appreciation
of the oneness of this vast universe.

We are one with everything,
living and nonliving,
on this planet,
connected, interrelated,
and interdependent,
as we share atoms, oxygen, and carbon dioxide.

And we are one with
the Source and Sustainer of all that exists,
the Spirit and Energizer
visible
in this vast body
in endless diversity.

We rejoice
in our human capacity

to wonder and marvel,
to appreciate,
to understand connectedness,
to respect diversity,
to seek meaning and purpose,
to rejoice,
and to give thanks.

We give thanks
for men and women
in many differing cultures and times
who spoke and wrote
about our connectedness
with each other,
with all of creation,
and with the Source of all that exists.

We give thanks
for scholars and scientists
who have led us to shape
new understandings
of our connectedness with everything that exists
and who have led us
to increased wonder and awe and reverence.

We give thanks for Jesus
and for all religious leaders
whose insights and teachings
about the reign of God in our midst
have stood the test of time

and open our eyes and minds
to our bonding with
the Spirit of Life and Love.
They challenge us
to allow that Spirit of Life
to be evident in our relatedness
with all that exists,
living and nonliving.

May we grow in respect
for religious differences
within our own religion
and among all religions.

May we think about,
reflect on,
and explore faith
with open minds
and freedom to move beyond where we are now,
so that we may accept the challenge
of shaping religious faith
that embraces all people
living in love
and living in God.

Living in Love

Earthen Vessels Holding Treasure

After the death of Jesus, Christians shaped their conviction that whoever lives in love lives in God and God lives in them. This conviction has special significance in the context of the New Story. Jesus did not create the link between living in love and living in God. No, it was always so. Anyone who has ever lived on earth has lived in God. Anyone who has ever loved has lived and loved in God — and God has lived and loved in them. Isaiah lived in love; Ruth lived in love; Buddha lived in love; Confucius lived in love. They lived and loved in God and God lived and loved in them. God came to expression in them, as in all people, as best God could, in personal giftedness, in personal limitations, and in the historical, cultural, and religious conditioning of the times.

God's Spirit has always been present and active in human activity. What Jesus did so wonderfully and clearly was to call people to reflect on the everyday expressions of their loving and to recognize the presence of God's Spirit within them as they cared, fed, visited,

Katie Odell

This Presence came to visible expression in the formation of stars and galaxies and planets, rocks and gasses, water and soil, living things and ourselves.

forgave, and shared. Jesus himself lived so lovingly that he revealed how God can come to wonderful expression in human form.

In this prayer we reflect on the wonder of life, love, God, Jesus, and who we are.

✠

We believe in a sustaining, life-giving Presence
active in our universe for all the billions of years
since the first moment of its existence.
Working within and with what was there,
this Presence came to visible expression
in the formation of stars
and galaxies
and planets,
rocks and gasses,
water and soil,
living things
and ourselves as a life-form
with conscious awareness and appreciation
of this Presence.

We marvel at life,
not knowing where and how it started
nor when and how it reached this planet.
We celebrate ourselves as a life-form giving
the Source of all that is
unique expression
in our awareness,

in our intelligence,
and in our ability to communicate.

In us, this Source can sing and dance,
write and speak,
love and create,
hold and nurture.

We give flesh and bone,
visible expression,
to this ultimate mystery.
We are earthen vessels that hold a treasure,
"works of art,"
"temples" of the Spirit of Life.

Throughout human history,
men and women have given wonderful expression to
    this Spirit
as they offered insights about human existence
and our connectedness
with the Source of all that exists.

Jesus is *the* story we gather around
and give thanks for.
Human like us,
he discerned where this Source is found:
in the everyday,
in human interaction,
in feeding,
in caring,
in clothing,

in visiting,
in sharing,
in forgiving,
in being neighbor.

He urged people
to work together to establish
the "reign of God"
by wholehearted generosity,
by eliminating boundaries between people,
by trust in the goodness of people,
and by working for peace and justice,
in all human endeavors.

We remember his total commitment
to living fully and loving totally
and his faith in a God to be trusted
whatever twists life could take in this imperfect world.

Confronted with failure, abandonment, and a
     humiliating death
Jesus remained faithful to his belief
in a constant and eternal connectedness
between human living and loving
and the Source of all existence.
He died in that belief,
and in a way we do not understand,
yet one day hope to share in,
he died *into* that Source,
into the Spirit that had come to visibility in him.

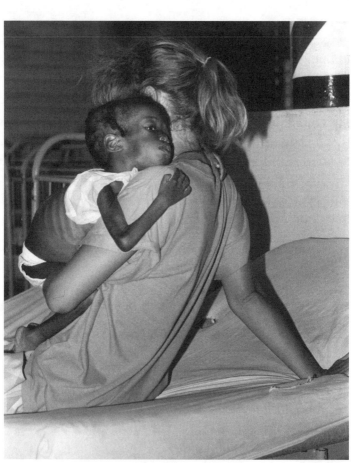

Mev Puleo

This Source is found: in the everyday, in human interaction, in feeding, in caring, in clothing, in visiting, in sharing, in forgiving, in being neighbor.

Gathered here to share bread
in memory of Jesus,
we give our "Amen"
to his belief
that when we live in love
we live in God and God lives and loves in us.

We break this bread:
Bread inviting us
to grasp what the eye cannot see:
God with us
in the journey of life;
God with us
in the ordinary
and the everyday;
God with us
in our living and loving.

We eat this bread
giving our Amen
to God
living and loving
in us.

We drink this wine,
wine reminding us
of promises to love,
of love generously shared,
of Jesus who loved so totally,
and our call

to love as courageously
as Jesus loved.

Time for quiet reflection: God lives and loves in me.

We give thanks for the Spirit of Life
visible in Jesus,
visible in us,
visible in people in all walks of life.
We give thanks for faith
that recognizes and names this presence
and this bonding of all people,
and we pray for
clearer naming
and recognition of this bonding
in our religion
and in all religions,
so that the peace
Jesus yearned for all people to experience
may one day be reality in our world.

We pray that we will allow the life and the teaching of
    Jesus
to motivate all that we do
so that what we profess to have seen in his life
and heard in his teaching
might be evident in our living and loving.

Jesus, Human Like Us

Setting Us Free

If we believe that God has always been present in the development of the human species, then our understanding of Jesus as someone who "saves" us takes on added meaning. Jesus "saves" us by "setting us free" from ideas and images suggesting that God is distant from our everyday living, that God is to be feared, that we have to win God's mercy or that God keeps a record of our sins and will punish us accordingly. Jesus sets us free from the religious bonds created by ideas of distance from God and the sense of fear.

Jesus, more like us than we ever really imagined, reveals to us the wonder of who we are as bearers of the Spirit of God.

✠

Human like us, Jesus allowed God's creative Spirit to move in him

~ in the days of his youth

~ in the days of young adulthood

~ in the days and nights of his searching and
  questioning

~ in his hopes and dreams of what could be

~ in shaping his understanding of where the sacred
  was to be found

~ in finding ways to free people from religious images
  and ideas that kept them captive and dependent
  and fearful of God

~ in moving away from religious institutionalism

~ in giving thanks to his God for the wonderful times
  in his life

~ in breaking down social and religious barriers

~ in challenging religious leaders to move beyond
  legalism

~ in being maligned and rejected and misunderstood

~ in enduring loneliness and disappointment

~ in giving his all in being neighbor to all

~ in his absolute conviction that human love and
  concern express the presence of the sacred

~ in walking in faith, with his doubts and questions
  and concerns about the future

~ in facing failure

~ in facing death.

Jesus died for what he believed.
He died
in shame and disgrace,

Jorge Fernandez

Living in love is living in God.

in pain and loneliness,
in failure and defeat,
but also in the conviction
that love is stronger than evil,
that God is present even in darkness and chaos,
that life is stronger than death,

that God is to be trusted absolutely,
that living in love is living in God,
that dying in love is dying into God,
and that resurrection and new life always follow death.

We remember the night before Jesus died
when he shared with his friends a sacred meal
commemorating God's constant presence
in both hard times and good times.
Knowing a hard time was coming
he took bread,
food for life's journey,
and wine,
recalling bonds and commitment,
and shared them,
asking his friends to remember him
whenever they met to share the meal.

So we break and share bread
and drink wine,
gladly remembering him
and pledging ourselves
to allow the Spirit that moved in him
to move freely in our lives.

Time for quiet reflection: Jesus, human like me.

Jesus, human like us,
reveals to us our true identity:
earthen vessels that hold a treasure,
temples of God's Spirit.

Jesus, human like us,
reveals God present and active
throughout human history.

Jesus, human like us,
reveals God-always-with-us
in our everyday loving.

Jesus, human like us,
challenges us
to let his story
be our story also.

We share the convictions of Jesus
and rejoice to be "church,"
followers of Jesus,
people set free
and in our freedom
called to share this good news with all people
who seek connection between human experience
and the Unknown Source and Sustainer we call "God."

Christmas

Emmanuel: God-Is-with-Us

Who is this child for us?

Yes, he is *God-with-us,* but in the New Story context we do not think about the birth of this child as an intervention into this world by an elsewhere God. We endeavor to see God as present everywhere, at all times, and Jesus as giving human expression to the God *always with us.*

Jesus is revealer of God in our midst. He challenges us to stop looking in the wrong places for the sacred. The Christmas story will always be the story of God-here-with-us in the ordinary, the everyday, the chaos, the shabbiness of a stable, the flight into exile, the love between a man and a woman, the birth of a child, and in people despised because of their lowly social status.

Our prayer invites us to recognize God's presence with us, especially in places we are reluctant to look.

✚

We believe in an Ultimate Reality,
a reality beyond our words

and beyond our images,
a reality that grounds and sustains everything that
    exists.

We see this Reality at work
in the immensity of our universe,
in the incredible display of life-forms on this planet
and in the development of consciousness
in the human species.

All our collected human wisdom
is a visible expression of this Reality,
active for millions of years
in human development
active in all places,
at all times,
in individuals and cultures,
seeking expression in the betterment of humanity.

As Christians we rejoice in the birth of Jesus.
In him we see the fullness of human possibility:
to make God visible in our lives.
In him we have seen the Ultimate Reality,
God, Breath of Life, Wisdom,
come to expression in human form.

Like all of us
he grew in wisdom as he aged.
He questioned,
he searched for meaning,
he shaped his convictions,

he experienced love
and came to know love's connectedness
with his God.

He stood firmly in his own religious tradition
and preached good news
to all people dreaming of
a better humanity.

We rejoice that his teaching sets us free
from imagining a manipulative, intervening God
and from thinking we are distant from the Reality
in which our very existence is grounded.

We rejoice that Jesus led people
to discover the sacred in the ordinary:
in the crowd,
in the lowly,
in everyday life,
in human yearnings to be better people,
and in being neighbor to one another.

We rejoice that his teaching
sets us free to believe
that we live *in* God
and that God lives
and comes to wonderful expression *in* us.
We believe in an eternal dimension
to this intimate connectedness,
giving meaning to who we are.

Robert McCahill

Our Christmas prayer is that we may recognize and actively
acknowledge the presence of the sacred in places we are
reluctant to look.

We are thankful for Jesus' courage
in the face of opposition
and powerful influences
wanting to silence him.

We remember the night before he died,
when he shared a meal with his friends.
He took bread,
honoring the God of faithful presence
in the ordinary
and in the ups and downs of life.

He gave thanks
for all the blessings in his life
and shared the bread with his friends,
asking them to gather in memory of him
and to live in a covenant of love
with their God.

We break bread
as Jesus broke bread,
mindful of the call to love generously and faithfully,
whatever the cost.

We eat this bread,
giving our "Amen"
to loving as Jesus loved.

We take wine,
mindful of our responsibility
to be bearers of forgiveness, tolerance, and
    understanding.

We drink,
committing ourselves
to allow the Spirit of generosity
that took flesh
and moved so boldly in Jesus
to move in our lives.
To this commitment we give our "Amen"
and offer it as our Christmas gift
to our family and friends
and neighbors.

*Time for quiet reflection: The Spirit of Generosity
    active in my life.*

We give thanks for God being with us
in the love from family and friends,
in whatever has been,
in the circumstances of life now,
and in whatever the future holds for us.

Our Christmas prayer is that we may recognize
and actively acknowledge
the presence of the sacred
in places we are reluctant to look:

~ in the stables of our own lives

~ among the downtrodden in our society

~ in refugees

~ in people who are different from us.

May we recognize God-in-us
and give generous expression
to this wonderful gift we all share.
Amen.

Good Friday

A Close Companion

Let us not lose sight of Jesus, who leads us in our faith.
—Hebrews 12:2

This prayerful reflection emphasizes the human experience of living in faith rather than any theological interpretation about the death of Jesus. This is the Jesus Christians must know better if they are to turn to him in times of pain, struggle, and darkness. Many Christians are still inclined to say, "But Jesus would not know what it is like to carry my pain or to have my doubts. He was God." We need much more prayerful reflection on the Jesus who *knows* the longings and the pains of the human heart before we theologize about him. Otherwise we run the risk of theologizing about someone who is not at all like the rest of us.

Reflection 1

I remember a man who had dreams of what might be:
that people would be set free from ideas and images
  about God that enslaved them,

that people would believe that through their everyday
acts of human kindness they are intimately
connected with the sacred,
that people would live "in peace, in God's presence,
all the days of their lives" (Luke 1:75).
I remember a man driven by his dreams.

Reflection 2

I remember a man who had his moments of
breakthrough,
when it must have seemed his dream was being
realized,
the times people really listened and responded,
the men and women who were prepared to walk with
him and support him,
times when he spoke better and more convincingly
than other times.
I remember a man enthused by his successes.

Reflection 3

I remember a man who learned of the cruel death of
his cousin.
He got into a boat, seeking a lonely place, where he
could be with his friends
to absorb the shock,
to grieve quietly,

and to calm the feelings
of powerlessness and frustration
and fear for his own future.
I wonder what he prayed about that night?
I wonder what helped him leave that lonely place and
    go forward to confront life, rather than retreat into
    isolation and safety?
I remember a man driven by his convictions.

Reflection 4

I remember a man who had to find quiet places to
    pray and think about things,
a man who had to live by faith,
a man who had to search for answers,
a man who had to think about which path to follow,
a man who looked to his friends for support and
    understanding.
I remember someone very much like me.

Reflection 5

I remember a man whose dream was shattered,
who broke down and cried over what could have been,
who knew the pain of failure and powerlessness,
who knew what it was like to feel broken and terribly
    alone.
I remember someone human like all of us.

Reflection 6

I remember a man who knew he was going to die,
who gathered with his friends knowing it was for the
 last time,
who spoke to them about what he really believed,
who wanted them to remember him and to keep his
 dream alive.
I remember a testament to love.

Reflection 7

I remember a man crucified.
He was a failure,
abandoned by his male friends,
taunted, despised,
enduring a shameful and agonizing death,
no consoling or heartfelt presence of his God to help
 him.
I remember a man whose faith in all he believed was
 tested to the limits.

Reflection 8

I remember a man who forgave,
not just once, but over and over,
a man who embodied the generosity and limitless
 outpouring of the Source of all life,

a man whose life and death point us to another
    dimension of what it means to be human.
No power on earth, nothing, could move this man
    from what he believed.
I remember a man who inspires me by the way he
    died.

Reflection 9

I remember a man of extraordinary religious insight,
utterly convinced of the connectedness
between human loving and living *in* God,
determined to give people personal authority in their
    relationship with God,
wanting to set people free from fear of the Unknown,
setting his heart on breaking down barriers between
    people.
I remember a man who sets me free.

We give thanks
for the ways
in which the life,
teaching,
and death
of Jesus
have set us free.

We open ourselves
to the influence of the Spirit of Life and Love
that moved so obviously in Jesus' life.

We want his convictions
and his dreams to live on in us.

Jesus challenges us to have faith and hope
when all seems lost,
so we turn our minds and hearts
to our world and we pray:

Let this be a time of silent prayer. Someone could mention a focus, for example, for families in the neighborhood struggling with grief or loss, for people suffering religious persecution, etc.

We break bread today
remembering Jesus,
who died for what he believed.
He died trusting in God's presence with him
in spite of darkness,
loneliness,
failure,
abandonment,
torment,
and pain.

We break this bread
mindful of faith
that sees beyond what the eye can see,
faith that endures,
faith that inspires,
~ Jesus' faith,
~ our faith.

Joseph W. Towle

We break this bread mindful of faith that sees beyond what the eye can see, faith that endures, faith that inspires.

We eat this bread
and give our Amen
to sharing the faith of Jesus.

We drink this wine
mindful of love's call
to be faithful,
to endure,
to bond,
to see possibilities and the hope of new life,
to be generous and forgiving whatever the cost.

Time for quiet reflection:
I remember Jesus who inspires me.

We give thanks for Jesus who "leads us in our faith."
We give thanks that Jesus knows the longings and
pains of our hearts.
We pray that we will grow strong in that faith in which
Jesus faced life and death.
We pray that he will be a close companion for us in
life and in death.
Amen.

Easter

New Beginnings

In nature we see superb aspects of transformation: in supernovas exploding and in their dying giving birth to new possibilities; in the sun giving of itself that we might have life; in seeds "dying" to produce new life. We know that several times in the history of this planet most species then existing were extinguished. There have been death, destruction, apparent annihilation, and then "resurrection" producing abundant life. Life is somehow stronger than death. Life finds a way.

Human death is the greatest mystery we face. As Christians, we look to the life, teaching, death, and resurrection of Jesus to throw light on the mystery for us. Death for Jesus was, as it will be for us, a dying *into* God: a transformation into a way of existence for which we have no images and no clear ideas of how it may happen. Our understanding of Jesus' resurrection must be freed from the dualistic images in which Scripture and traditional Christian teaching have presented it. God does not reside somewhere else, in a place called "heaven" that is above us somewhere. In fact, there is no up or down any more when we consider our planet's place in the universe. Death for us will not be a journey to some other place where God is located; there will not be a judgment as to whether we "get into" an elsewhere place.

We proclaim and celebrate Easter because it links Jesus with all life, with transformation, and with possibility of life beyond our imagining. Easter offers meaning and hope to all people. We give thanks and rejoice that Jesus so clearly and courageously linked our loving and our dying with living on in God. We rejoice that Jesus lives on, as we all will, in the reality we call God.

✤

We believe
that death
is not the end,
but rather
a transformation
into new possibilities.

Nothing that exists
is ever completely destroyed.
A star exploding
or a leaf falling:
both offer new possibilities
and will "live on"
in ways unknown to stars and leaves.

Winter gives way to Spring;
what seemed lifeless
now abounds with life,
new possibilities and delights.

> We, too, experience
> new possibilities
> arising from our failures
> or disappointments
> or what has come to an end.

✠

We give thanks
for all the influences in our lives
that have helped us see beyond the present
and have called us to live in hope and trust
whatever endings we have experienced.

We give thanks for Jesus of Nazareth
for leading us to put our hope and trust
in the Spirit of Life and Love
moving in the depths of our being.

We give thanks
for the way he opened our minds and hearts
to see and appreciate the intimate and never-ending
    connection
between our loving
and the Spirit of Love.

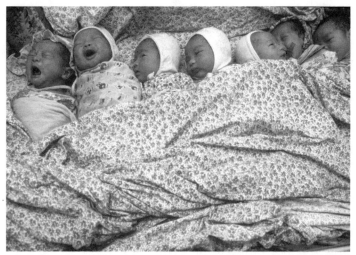

Richard Lord

We give thanks for the Spirit of New Life.

We give thanks
for the Spirit of New Life
active in our lives
as it was in the life of Jesus.

At this Easter gathering,
we take bread,
as Jesus took bread,
and we remember,
as Jesus remembered,
the constant presence
of the Spirit of Life and Love.

We break
and share this bread,
as Jesus broke and shared it.
We share it
as our pledge of openness
to the Spirit in our midst,
and in acknowledgment
of our eternal connectedness
with the Spirit of Life.

We take wine
and drink,
as Jesus invited his friends to drink,
mindful of a relationship of love and trust
between ourselves and the Spirit of Life,
believing,
as Jesus believed,
that beyond pain and darkness and death,
life in the Spirit continues
in ways beyond our imagining.

Time for quiet reflection:
I am eternally linked with the Source of all life.

To being the Body of Christ
and to being open
to the Spirit of New Life
in our lives
and in our world:
Amen.

For the journey that life has been,
for all that life is for us now,
for all that the future holds,
and for the mystery of life beyond death:
Amen.

Pentecost

At All Times, in All Places

Pentecost, in the context of the New Story, is not the story of Jesus ascending to "heaven" in order to send the Spirit upon us. Rather it is the wonderful story of God's Spirit always present, always active in human development and given total and free expression in human form by Jesus of Nazareth.

It is the amazing story of people coming to awareness through reflection on the life of Jesus that the same Spirit that moved in him moved in them. They realized it was now their responsibility to give witness to the Spirit in their lives as totally and as freely as Jesus had.

Pentecost is the wonderful good news that all people who live in love live in God and God lives in them.

Pentecost presents a challenge to humanity: What would life on earth be like if the actions of all people were motivated by their awareness of being "temples of God's Spirit"?

✠

We believe in a Spirit
that holds together all that exists,
that is Mind in all things,
that sustains connectedness and relationships in all
    things.

We believe in a Spirit
that works in and through what it has to work with,
in space beyond our comprehension,
in billions of galaxies,
in disintegrations and in new beginnings,
constantly creating new possibilities,
in stars that shrank and exploded and produced the
    atoms that form our bodies,
in gases gravitating together to form planets.

We believe in a Spirit that emerged into visibility
in the first life-forms that appeared on earth,
and then in diversity beyond our imagining,
in the first flowers and plants,
in the first animals,
in the first inhabitants of the oceans,
in the widespread destruction of life on this planet
long, long before human life emerged,
in the new beginnings that emerged from destruction,
in the first humanoids to use fire and make their own
    clothes,
in the first humans who struggled to communicate,
in the development of language and ideas,
in humankind's search for meaning,

development of culture,
in looking to gods to explain the unexplainable,
in the growth of philosophy and human wisdom,
in people in all parts of this world who articulated a
   worthwhile understanding of human existence and
   purpose,
in Isaiah, Ruth, Naomi, Buddha, and Zoroaster,
in matriarchal and patriarchal religions,
in the goodness and in the limitations and the
   mistakes of religious beliefs.

Jesus of Nazareth embodied this Spirit so wonderfully
that he became like a mirror to us,
showing us of what we are capable
when we allow this same Spirit
to work freely in our lives.

We remember Jesus
grateful for his light and inspiration
in the human search for meaning
and concern for the betterment of humanity.
We are grateful for insights assuring us that:
We are temples of God's Spirit.
We are earthen jars that hold a treasure.
We are God's work of art.
Our loving is intertwined
with the Spirit of Love.
The Spirit of Love lives in us.
Perfect love casts out fear.
Love never ends.

We are temples of God's Spirit.
We are earthen jars that hold a treasure.
We are God's work of art.

We pray
that people may see in us
the courage and the generosity
that characterized Jesus' life
as we pledge ourselves
to be embodiments
of the Spirit he bore
and of the dream he dreamed.
May people see in us
what we profess to have seen in him —
the Spirit alive in our midst.

Like Jesus we will work
to create the "reign" of God
in our work for justice and peace,
to break down barriers between people,
to profess all people are filled with the one Spirit,
to put an end to religious elitism
and religious wars.

With glad hearts
we gather in memory of Jesus.
We break and share bread
as a sign of our awareness
of the Spirit always with us
in all we do
and as a sign of our commitment
to love generously and wholeheartedly.

We drink wine
in joyful recognition
of a Spirit poured out
into our world and into our lives
and in gratitude
for the gifts we each have
and are called to share.

Pause for quiet reflection:
The Spirit of Life and Love lives in me.

May the Spirit within us
be a source of healing and consolation.

May the Spirit within us
strengthen us when we feel weak,
warm us when we are cold-hearted,
bend us when we are stubborn,
move us when we are uncaring,
guide us in the way of love.

May the Spirit within us
shine in all we do.

—Adapted from the Pentecost Sequence

Celebrating Family

Breaking Bread Together

They met in their houses for the breaking of bread; they
shared their food gladly and generously.
— Acts of the Apostles 2:46

The early Christian practice of house gatherings con-
tinued the Jewish prayer custom of gathering to remember and to tell the story of God-with-them.

This is a prayer for family gatherings. It makes use of
the familiar symbols of bread and wine in accord with
the earliest custom of Christians gathering recorded in
Scripture.

✠

We gather in the belief
that in being
male and female,
husband, wife,
mother, father,
daughter, son,
brother, sister,
relation, friend,

90

Eric Wheater

We trust the power of Love in our lives.

we give the Source and Sustainer of all that exists
wonderful ways
of coming to expression.

With the gift of awareness,
we acknowledge and rejoice in
the treasures each of us holds:
intelligence, love,
memory, imagination,
our plans and hopes and dreams,
our individual talents,
our relationships that nurture and sustain us,
our freedom,
and our opportunities for personal development.

We give thanks for Jesus,
who enlightened us
and opened our eyes
to the presence of the Spirit of Life
in our everyday "treasures"
and led us to acknowledge
the intimate connection
between "living in love and living in God."

We give thanks
for Jesus' insistence
that we trust the power of Love
in our lives
and face life with hope
whatever happens.

Marty Costello

We give thanks for all that we mean for each other.

We rejoice
as Jesus often rejoiced,
in the simple pleasure of
sharing a meal with family and friends.

We give thanks
for the years of bonding,
for respect and sensitivity
to differences among us,
for affirmation and encouragement,
for generous sharing and mutual support,
and for all that we mean for each other.

Name particular blessings for which you are thankful.

We share this bread and wine
and let them speak to us,
as Jesus let them speak to him,
of what the eye cannot see:

~ commitment

~ relationships

~ sharing

~ memories

~ gratitude

~ healing

~ hopes.

We eat and drink with deep gratitude
for the blessings in our lives
and who we are for one another.

Bread and wine are shared.

We give thanks for all that has been
and for all we are for each other.
May the bonds of our loving
continue to strengthen
as we each face whatever life holds for us.
May we always be for each other
real expressions of the "body of Christ."
Amen.

Eucharist

Giving Thanks in the Twenty-first Century

What might a "eucharistic prayer" look like if we focused on ideas and images in tune with contemporary knowledge about our universe? This prayer is a modified version of the prayer in *Is Jesus God? Finding Our Faith.* *

✠

We give thanks
for the wonderful gift of reflective awareness
that allows us to recognize and name
the presence
of a Creator Spirit beyond all imagining
in our universe.

Everything we have,
everything we see,
everything we do,
everyone we love and everyone who loves us

---

*Michael Morwood, *Is Jesus God? Finding Our Faith* (New York: Crossroad, 2001), 118–20.

reveals this Sustaining Presence
and our total dependence on it.

We marvel and wonder at the size and complexity of
    our universe.
We marvel and wonder at the development of life on
    this planet.
We give thanks for the Creative Presence that
    "charges" this life and all that exists.
We recognize that human life gives this Creator Spirit
a particular way of coming to expression,
and that in us the Spirit can sing and dance,
speak and write, love and create.

Conscious that we live, move, and have our being
in this Spirit,
we give thanks for people throughout history
who have affirmed this loving presence in all people
and who have challenged people
to give witness to this
by lives characterized by mercy, gratitude,
compassion, generosity, and forgiveness.

We give thanks for Jesus of Nazareth,
who loved so greatly
and taught so clearly and courageously
that he was able to set people free
from images and ideas and religious practices
that bound them into fear and a false sense of
    separation from the Spirit of all Life.

Through him we have learned
how our loving is a sharing in the life of this Spirit.
In him we see the Spirit of Life challenging all of us
to make its presence on earth more visible.

We remember the night before he died,
when he took bread,
gave thanks for everything he had,
broke the bread and shared it with his friends
asking them to remember his total surrender
to the Spirit of Life and Love
and his enduring love for each of them.
We take this bread and eat it,
mindful of the Spirit at work in our lives,
in the ordinary,
in the everyday,
and in our desire to love
as generously as Jesus loved.

Likewise, knowing his life was to be poured out,
Jesus shared the cup of wine with his friends.
We drink now,
mindful of our bonding with Jesus
and with all people
through the Spirit at work in our lives.

We believe that like all people who lived in love and
    died in love
Jesus died into the Creator Spirit's eternal loving
    embrace.

We are thankful that his story grounds our belief
in eternal, loving connectedness with the Spirit of Life
and with all our relatives and friends who have died.

We pray for all who allow the mind and heart and
    spirit of Jesus
to motivate their actions.
We pray that Christian leadership may be
open and affirming,
creative and challenging.
We pray that all Christians
might better recognize, acknowledge, and acclaim
the Creative Spirit's presence in all people,
at all times, in all places.

For ourselves gathered here we ask the grace
to be who and what we ritualize here:
the "body of Christ,"
people committed by our "Amen"
to allowing this Spirit to move freely in our lives.
We give thanks that we have gathered here
as the body of Christ.
We rejoice in the giftedness of each person here.
We are grateful for who we are for each other.
We consider ourselves blessed
in and *by* the Creative Spirit.
May we be truly eucharistic in all we do.
To this prayer we give our Amen.

In Time of Tragedy

Where Is God?

Life has a way of testing what we really believe. Life tested Jesus. What do you believe about God when powerful people murder your cousin? What motivates you to keep on hoping for change in people when you experience isolation and rejection? What do you believe about God when you are nailed to a cross and all your dreams seem to have crumbled into nothing?

Jesus knew what it was like to be in darkness, to feel isolated, to need to pray about things and make sense of what was happening in his life. In times of loss, pain, and tragedy we can turn to him because he knows what it is like to be in our shoes. He has been there. We can turn to him for the healing that comes from compassion, from being understood.

Jesus preached the importance of living in a trusting relationship with God, free from notions of a God ready to hand out physical misfortune, loss, or death as a punishment for sin.

The New Story can lead us into a deeper appreciation of Jesus' teaching. God is not an overseer,

directing circumstances from elsewhere. God is intimately *in* the pain with us; we are living *in* God.

✙

We look to the life and death of Jesus
for strength and hope
in this time of tragedy.

With the conviction of Jesus
we believe that
whatever the pain,
whatever the loss,
our God is here in the midst of our suffering,
our God is not distant,
our God is not a Divine manipulator,
our God is Life-Giver.

We remember
how life tested Jesus' conviction,
when
in suffering,
in failure,
in loneliness,
in powerlessness,
in darkness,
in pain,
and in disappointment
he never abandoned his belief
in God's presence with him.

Jesus,
like so many people
before and after him,
showed the depth
of the human spirit
in its capacity
to love, to trust,
and to hope.

Jesus invites us
to name this spirit
as the Spirit of God
at work in our lives.
Jesus reveals to us
our connectedness
with the Ground and Source
of all life,
in our loving,
our trusting,
and our hoping.

Whenever we take bread,
as Jesus took bread
on the night before he died,
we remember God-with-us
in all the ups and downs of life
and we commit ourselves,
as Jesus committed himself,
to love and trust and hope
whatever the circumstances of life.

When we drink wine
in memory of Jesus
in times of tragedy or loss,
we recall his faithfulness
when life tested him
and we draw hope and courage from him
and from all people
who allow the Spirit of Love
to be stronger than despair, cynicism, and isolation.

Time for quiet, prayerful support for someone.

We give thanks especially
for friends
who support and sustain us
in difficult times,
and we drink,
mindful of God's Spirit
at work in each of us.

May that Spirit clearly
love,
trust,
and hope
in us.
We believe
that the power of God's Spirit
at work in us
can do far more than we can ask
or imagine. (Eph. 3:20)

Marriage — A Reading

The Spirit of Life and Love in Human Form

You are a man and woman of love.
You bring to this wedding ceremony
all that you are
and all that has made you who you are:
your families, your friends,
your giftedness,
your experiences of life,
your insights, and your wisdom.
You bring your hopes and your dreams
of what shared love might be.

In your love for each other
we see the Spirit of Love and Life
in human form
and we rejoice,
in the wonderful ways each of you
makes that Spirit visible to us.

Be always the man and the woman you are
because that is what delights and attracts you
and brings you together.

It is also what we,
your family and friends,
delight in.

But let there also be space and room
for the other to grow
as you form a bond this day
that you wish to be unending and unbreakable.

May that bonding be joyful and gracious.
May your love be overflowing and generous.

In all the years to come
may you delightedly be
N and N (*insert names of bride and groom*),
wife and husband,
strong and constant in love
for each other,
for your families,
and for your friends.

Wedding Anniversary

Celebrating God's Presence in Our Loving

A wedding anniversary offers a wonderful occasion for blending and praying the best of the traditional Christian story and the New Story. We can blend the symbols of bread and wine and the words of Scripture with the conviction that God's creative Spirit at work throughout the entire universe for billions of years has come to expression in the lives and love shared by this couple.

✛

Friends to couple:
Do you realize
that you are temples
of God's holy Spirit
and the Spirit of God is living in you? (1 Cor. 3:16)

Couple:
We realize that
we are indeed temples
of God's holy Spirit,
and that our loving

is a certain sign of
the Spirit of God living within us.

> *Friends*:
> You have bonded together in love.
> Do you believe that
> to live in love is to live *in* God
> and for God to live *in* you? (1 John 4:16)

Couple:
We believe that God has no greater way
to manifest love for
and presence with
each of us (and our family)
than the love that binds our lives together.
We live and love in God,
and God lives and loves in us.

All:
We celebrate
the presence of the Spirit of Life and Love
at work in all places, at all times
throughout this vast universe
and in the development of life on earth.

We celebrate
the Spirit coming to expression
in men and women
in so many different cultures
and religions
throughout human history.

We celebrate
and give thanks for
the men and women
through the ages
who have recognized in human love
a connecting thread
with the mystery behind all life and all love.

We give thanks for Jesus of Nazareth
who so clearly named this connectedness for us
leading us to move beyond fear of the mystery
and moving us to trust that
our loving is the surest sign
of God's presence and "reign"
in our lives and in our world.

We remember the night Jesus spoke of his love for his
    friends,
when he took bread,
mindful of God's constant presence in his life,
gave thanks for that presence,
and shared the bread with his friends,
wanting them to remember
his own faithful love
and his belief in the bond between human and divine
    love.

We break
and share this bread,
as Jesus broke and shared it,

Dorothy Day, Marquette University Archives

What the Spirit brings is love, joy, peace, patience, kindness, goodness, trustfulness, gentleness.

and we give it to one another
as our pledge of openness to the Spirit of Love in our
  midst
and as our remembrance of Jesus,
who enlightened our minds and hearts
and who was ready to die for what he believed.

We take this wine
and drink,
as Jesus asked his friends to drink,
mindful of a relationship of love and trust
between ourselves and the Spirit of Life,
believing,
as Jesus believed,
that to live in love is to live in God
and to have God live and love in us.

After a time of quiet reflection, someone reads:

What the Spirit brings is
love, joy,
peace, patience,
kindness, goodness,
trustfulness, gentleness,
and self-control. (Gal. 5:22)

*Those present are then invited to name the ways they
see the Spirit of Love active in the life of the couple.*

*After this sharing, the couple renew their marriage
vows.*

Death

Living on in God

In memory of Patricia Heskett

What happens in death? This remains one of the questions most asked by Christians who have abandoned dualistic images of heaven and earth and images of souls leaving this place of "exile" and going "home" to heaven. Those images gave comfort and assurance, but for people embracing a different worldview, death is more mysterious than ever and there are no clear images. We believe we live *in* God and that death will be a transformation into another way of existing on *in* God.

The following reflections, in memory of Patricia Heskett, invite consideration of death in light of the New Story. They may lead us to a significantly different way of praying at the funeral and the gravesite or crematorium.

Reflection 1

We believe we exist *in* God, a God beyond our images and descriptions, a God beyond the many names we use: Universal Mind, Breath of Life, Creator, Source and Sustainer of everything that exists.

We believe the God in whom we exist is present in every part of this vast universe.

Everywhere we look this Energizing Presence comes to visible expression. We believe that each of us gives this Presence and Source a unique way of doing so.

Everywhere we look we can observe the perpetual rhythm of new life, followed by death, followed by new life. So we do not believe that death is the final end of anything, nor is it for us the start of a journey to somewhere else.

Rather, it is a transformation and a continuation of the ebb and flow of existence in ways we do not understand.

Every atom in Pat's body was produced in the unimaginable explosion of a distant star billions of years ago. And every atom in her body will live on for millions and millions of years yet, whatever happens to this planet.

Reflection 2

There is mystery here
and we open ourselves to this mystery as we accept
    the reality of Pat's death.
Pat's death speaks to us
of the wonder of being human
in a universe so vast and so magnificent

and of our existence within a mystery and a power
that we cannot understand or put into words.
In a very real sense this vast and magnificent universe
    of ours
came alive and became aware in Pat.
She gave God a way of coming to expression,
here in our lives,
here in a way that reached out and touched us,
as daughter, wife, mother, grandmother, sister,
    relation, or loyal friend.
She lived and loved *in* God,
God lived and loved in her,
and in death she lives on in God.

Reflection 3

We remember how Jesus of Nazareth, by the way he
lived and died and by what he believed, led us to
recognize and name our intimate connectedness with
God in our everyday actions of human caring and loving. He inspired us to walk trustingly in life with God,
the Source of all life. And he showed us how to face
death — not with fear of the unknown, but with faith
and trust that love has an eternal dimension to it. We
believe that, like Jesus, Pat lives on in God, the Source
of all.

We believe, too,
that she will "live on,"
especially in Des,

Gary and Julie,
Janet and John,
Neil and Philippa,
in her grandchildren,
and in all of us who loved her so dearly
and who will miss her so greatly.

Pause

Let us pray:
We give thanks for the many ways Pat's life touched
    ours.
We give thanks for the generosity of her loving
~ an outpouring of God's love in human form.
We give thanks for her faithfulness
~ a mirror to us of God's constant presence with us.
We give thanks for her laughter and sense of fun and
    delight in life
~ the Breath of Life moved freely in her.
We give thanks for the ways Pat mothered, nurtured,
    encouraged, and supported
~ truly, God was here among us.
We give thanks for the courage with which she faced
    illness and death
~ the human spirit has extraordinary depth to it.

We pray that the Spirit of Life that moved so
    wonderfully in Pat's life
will find hopeful and generous expression in our lives.

We pray for those most touched by Pat's death.
May the Spirit of life and hope
emerge in their lives as
the Spirit of growth.
And may we,
who love them dearly,
embody the Spirit in our tenderness, care, and
    generosity.
Amen.

Final Prayer at the Crematorium or Gravesite

Where Am I Now?

Reflection

Do you know
that every atom
in my body,
here before you,
was manufactured
in a massive explosion
in a star
billions of years ago?

Do you believe,
as I do,
in a Spirit of Life at work
for billions of years
that finally brought human form
to those atoms?

In me
the Spirit of Life and Love
came to visible expression
in human form
when I loved you,
when I called you my friends,
when I laughed, when I cried,
when I did whatever you loved about me.

Where am I now?

I continue to dance
with the Spirit of Life and Love
in ways beyond
words and images.

But I am with you,
and always will be
as this Spirit
continues to move in your lives.

I am with you,
and always will be,
in the Spirit of Life and Love.

Presider:
Pat left this body on the day she died.
Let us say this final prayer together,
believing that Pat lives on
in the minds and hearts and lives of her family and
    friends.

Let us pray, believing also,
that Pat now lives on in the Spirit of Life and Love
that we call God.

As the coffin is moved the prayer begins.

All:
We take leave of Pat's body
in the belief that she lives on
in the Spirit of Life and Love
so evident in her life among us.

We take leave,
grateful
for the many wonderful ways
she allowed the Spirit of Life and Love
to be expressed in human form.

In her life we saw
the Breath of Life
become human.

In her death we believe
the woman we greatly loved
enters into the fullness
of the Breath of Life.

May all that we loved about her
continue to find expression
in the ways we love one another
and face whatever the future holds.
Amen.

All Saints

We Are All One in God

We believe in a "communion of saints." We believe that in death we are transformed into a new way of living on *in* God. We also believe that here and now we are living *in* God. Those who have died and we who are still living are all living *in* God. It is not as if we are here and they are somewhere else ("heaven"), which is what our imagination keeps telling us. No, we all exist in God and just as we imagine God to be present to us, then all that is of God is somehow present to us. If we believe the Spirit of God prays in us, if we believe that the earthen vessels we are give God a way of coming to expression, then all who have died into the reality of God are part of that prayer and expression.

✜

We pray,
raising our minds and hearts
to the mystery we name God,
always creatively active
throughout the universe,

on this wonderful planet,
in the slow development of life-forms here on earth,
and in the wonder of human life.

We pray
believing
our prayer
gives expression
to the presence of God
with us.

We pray
aware
we are in communion with
all men and women
throughout human history
who ever raised their minds and hearts
in prayer
to the mystery we call God.

We give thanks
for the insights about God
we have gained
from prayerful people
from various times, places, cultures, and religions.

We recognize
the Spirit of one God
at work in all places,
in all people,
at all times.

We are all one in God.

We believe our oneness extends beyond death:
that all who live *in* God
die *into* God
and are connected now
with us as we live in God.

We give thanks for Jesus,
who allowed the presence of God
to move so freely and generously in his life
that in him
we have seen a true picture of ourselves:
temples of God's Spirit,
earthen vessels carrying a treasure,
God expressed in human form.

We give thanks that through Jesus
we are set free from
magic and superstition,
fear of God
and the sense of distance from God.

We remember Jesus sharing his last meal,
asking his friends to love as he had loved,
to remember him whenever they met to tell the story
    of God in their lives.
So we take this bread,
as Jesus took bread,
and we give thanks
for the wonder of God in and with us,

and we eat,
committing ourselves
to love as Jesus loved,
wholeheartedly,
generously,
compassionately,
so that people will see expressed in us
what we have seen expressed in Jesus:
God-with-us.

We take this wine,
and we remember Jesus drinking wine with his
   friends.
We drink,
giving our "Yes"
to being on earth
the heart of God.

Time for quiet reflection:
I am one with all the "saints."

We give thanks
for Christians who have allowed
the message of Jesus
to find generous expression in their lives
and have sought to make the reign of God
visible on earth.

We give thanks
for men and women
of all religious beliefs

who have allowed
the Spirit of God
to work freely and generously
in their lives.

We pray that our awareness
of connectedness with Jesus
and all people
and all that exists
may expand our hearts and minds
and allow the Spirit of all Life
to move more freely in us.

We pray this
for ourselves,
for our church congregations,
for our country,
and for all of humanity.
Amen.

Praying What We Read

Turning Thoughts into Prayer

The insights and new understanding we gain from reading about the New Story can readily form the basis of our shared prayer. Take, for example, the following passage from Bede Griffiths. His portrayal of "mind" present in all matter leads him to a wonderful insight about who we are. The prayer that follows is an example of how that insight can be brought to prayer. It is offered with encouragement to readers: try composing your own prayers using a similar pattern. The more prayers we have and the more we share them with one another, the more our faith will be nurtured and our prayer enriched.

A Reading from Bede Griffiths, *A New Vision of Reality*

There is an organizing power at every level and this organizing power has the character of a mind. Mind, it has been said, reveals itself as "a pattern of self-organization and a set of dynamic relationships." In this sense it can be said that mind is present in matter from the beginning. . . . It creates order. It causes the self-organization of all organic structures and creates a set of dynamic relationships. So mind is present in matter, and in plants and animals, and that mind becomes conscious in us. And so in a very exact sense, it can be said that matter becomes conscious in human beings. This process which has been going on from the beginning of time becomes conscious in us.

It evolves into consciousness. We are at that stage of evolution at which the material universe is emerging into consciousness in each one of us.*

✠

We gather here
aware we live in a time of transition
for religious language and imagery
as we learn more and more
about our world and our universe.

Whatever holds everything in this universe together,
from the magnificence of galaxies
to electrons rushing within atoms,
we believe we are a life-form that brings
this Source and Sustainer,
Organizing Power, Mind,
to unique and wonderful expression.

---

*Bede Griffiths, *A New Vision of Reality* (London: Fount Paperbacks, 1992), 259–60.

John J. Beeching

We want to acknowledge and celebrate the mystery and wonder of who we are.

Aware of our uniqueness in this universe
as a conscious life-form
appreciating connectedness and mind at work
in all that exists,
we want to acknowledge and celebrate
the mystery and wonder of who we are
and to accept the responsibilities that come with it.

We are mindful of people throughout human history
who have opened our minds
to a deeper appreciation
of what it means to be human
and our connectedness with all of creation.

These lives and insights challenge us
and call us to be open to life and love
in all that we do,
with special regard
for generosity and forgiveness,
for awareness of our bonding with all people
for responsibility to care for this planet
and for appreciation that we are children of this
    universe.

We give thanks for Jesus
whose insights
have led us to believe
that our living and loving give tangible expression
to God who is Life,
Love,

Mind,
Cause and Sustainer of all that exists.

We take this bread,
as Jesus took bread,
and we give thanks,
as he gave thanks,
for life's journey with God.

We break and eat this bread,
expressing our willingness to love as Jesus loved,
so that what we respect most in him
may find expression in our lives.

We take wine,
as Jesus took wine,
mindful of our bonding
with God and with all that exists,
and we commit ourselves
to loving inclusively
and generously.

*Time for quiet reflection: The material universe
emerges into consciousness in me.*

We give thanks for who we are:
~ matter become conscious
~ the universe coming to reflect on itself
~ earthen vessels that hold a treasure
~ temples of God's Spirit
~ the body of Christ.

We rejoice in this awareness of ourselves.
We accept its responsibilities.
We will work with the Spirit that moved so evidently in
    Jesus' life
to make God's "reign" evident
in our lives and in our world.
Amen.

Prayer of Petition

Creating Ripples

Prayer is so much more than telling an elsewhere God what is going on and asking, petitioning this elsewhere God to intervene. Prayer is about "raising the mind and heart" to God — the God present with us in the depths of our being and present everywhere in the expansiveness of this universe.

While we may be unsure how God "hears" our prayer, we believe that the Spirit of God at work in and among us "can do more than we can ask or imagine" (Eph. 3:20).

We know that when we raise minds and hearts in prayer to the Presence within and among us extraordinary things happen. *How* this happens is quite a mystery to us. Love expressed *here* has an effect on love expressed *there*. While skeptics may scoff, there is plenty of evidence — for example "distance healing" with hospital patients — to show this does happen. There is also the fact that quantum physics reveals a similar mysterious world in which something *here* has an effect *there*. In ways we do not yet understand, all of reality is connected even across enormous distances.

Mind, as Bede Griffith suggests, is present everywhere as a "pattern of self-organization" and becomes conscious in us. This may be our best clue to some understanding of prayer of petition. It is not that we are trying to connect with a Supreme Being external to our world. Rather we are trying to allow mind to work in and among us. We are consciously tapping into mind (or Mind) in which we are all connected, but how the connection works is every bit as mysterious as quantum physics.

Seen in this new light, prayer of petition has hardly begun in the Western world. We have been too conditioned to asking the external God to intervene. We have been obsessed with "correct thinking," with logic, and with what our senses proclaim as real. The challenge now is to bring the concerns we raise in prayer to a different format (not addressing an elsewhere God) and to a different understanding of what we are trying or wanting to do when we share these concerns prayerfully: create ripples in the unifying mind in which we all have existence, so that reality is effected somewhere else.

We should be more serious about this type of prayer rather than dismiss it or trivialize it by praying for better weather or a win for our football team or success in exams.

Yes, let us pray for someone's good health or for a cure or for an end to warmongering or more compassion in political and religious leaders. This prayer can be effective whether the people being prayed for know this or not. Let us also make evident in our prayer that we are not closing our minds to the suffering in our world or to the social evils of our times. And let our prayers challenge us to *give expression* to God's presence in our world and in our homes.

When composing prayers of petition it is preferable to avoid the common usage of "that" statements, as in, "Let us pray for world leaders that...," "Let us pray for Mary Smith that...," with "Lord, hear us" and a response such as "Lord, hear our prayer" at the end of each statement. Rather, invite people to pray for a few moments in silence with invitations like the following:

✠

Let us pray for our bishop...

Let us raise our minds to the reality of HIV/AIDS in Africa...

Let us be present in prayer to sick people in our parish...

Let us pray for the men and women fighting the bushfires...

Let us pray for world peace...

The period of prayer could conclude as follows:

We pray these prayers in the belief
that we are bonded
in God's Spirit
with everything that exists.
We pray with faith and confidence.
Amen.

Gathering Prayer for a Faith-Sharing Group

Acknowledging the Spirit of Wisdom in Us

Traditional gathering prayer asks God to "send the Spirit" upon us for this meeting, gathering, or liturgy. How do we shape our gathering prayer if we no longer imagine God is somewhere else hearing our prayer and deciding to send the Spirit because we asked? We pray acknowledging God's Spirit here with us. We pray acknowledging the wonder of who we are. We pray acknowledging our responsibility to give expression to the Spirit of God in the best way we can.

✠

We gather
conscious that the Spirit of Wisdom
moves in each of us
as it has moved in all people
since the beginning of human life,
working in and through
whom and what it has to work with.

133

May we be wise in our sharing,
ready to listen,
open to learning where new insights and knowledge
    may take us,
drawing on wisdom that stands the test of time,
and courageous enough to discard whatever can no
    longer sustain our faith.

We pray that our gathering
may allow the Spirit of Wisdom
to be expressed here
as graciously
and as clearly
as is humanly possible.
Amen.

Reconciliation

A Different Sense of Sin

Reconciliation is not about restoring relations with a vengeful God who requires a supreme price to be paid before dispensing forgiveness. Reconciliation is about mending the bonds we break and the disruption we cause when we refuse to allow the Spirit of Graciousness and Generosity to be expressed in what we think, do, and say.

We acknowledge here in prayer, alone or with others, our constant connectedness with God, with all human beings, and with all that exists. We acknowledge the pain and hurt that come when we act as if we were disconnected. We acknowledge our responsibility for this disconnectedness and profess our readiness to heal, to mend, and to work for reconciliation.

✠

God,
creatively active
for billions of years in this emerging universe,
comes to expression in us.

In us,
God can be
generous,
loving,
creative,
happy,
delighted,
sad,
and disappointed
as
nowhere else.

God loves in us;
God cares through us;
God laughs in us;
God cries in us
as
nowhere else.

We are privileged
to know
this connectedness with God.

We are privileged
to give God
human expression.

We give thanks for Jesus
and for all people
who have opened our minds
to this understanding of who we are.

We give thanks for Jesus
and for all people
who have taught
and shown us
how to live
what we believe:
we are to act justly;
we are to walk humbly with our God;
we are to love our neighbor as ourselves;
we are to expand our notions of neighbor;
we are to care for all of material creation;
we are to forgive and be merciful;
we are to give God's Spirit freedom to act in us;
we are to make the "reign" of God evident in our
    world;
we are to love as Jesus would love — generously and
    wholeheartedly.

We express our sorrow
for the limits we have put
on God's Spirit at work in us,
by our unbelief and lack of understanding
of God's presence in us,
by acting as if we were disconnected
from God, our neighbor, and our world,
by our deliberate words and actions that have
ruptured connectedness,
and by our lack of concern
for social justice and environmental issues.

Quiet reflection: How is disconnectedness experienced — personally, socially?

~ in what way do my words and actions cause disconnectedness?

~ to what action does my reflection urge me?

~ to whom should I say "sorry"?

~ from whom should I ask forgiveness?

~ where do I see disconnectedness (injustice) socially?

~ what can I do about it?

We open our minds and hearts
to the presence of God in us.
May God-in-us
find generous and courageous expression
in our words and actions
as we undertake
to make the reign of God
evident in our world.
Amen.

Led by the Spirit

The Test of Genuine Prayer

Luke's Gospel (4:1) describes Jesus as "filled with the Holy Spirit, . . . led by the Holy Spirit" as he began the task of discerning his future. A few verses later, we read that "Jesus, with the power of the Spirit in him, returned to Galilee" (4:14) and began his public ministry.

Somewhere in his prayer and reflection, Jesus became convinced that he was "filled with the Holy Spirit" and possessed the "power of the Spirit" in him. The courageous step he took in life was to allow himself to be "led by the Holy Spirit" wherever that Spirit might take him.

Here is the true measure of our prayer. How willing are we to let ourselves be freely led by the Presence and Power within us? The best answer to "How do we pray now?" is: any way we can deepen our awareness of this Presence and Power within us; any way our prayer leads us to be as courageous as Jesus.

✠

In gathering here
we acknowledge
the presence
within and among us
of a Spirit,
present in all places
at all times
in this vast universe.

We acknowledge this Spirit
as the Source and Sustainer
of everything that exists,
bonding all things
in relationship
and connectedness,
a Spirit of constant movement
and new possibilities.

We marvel
at the way this Spirit
came to expression
on this planet,
especially in human life-form,
a life-form giving this Spirit
unique ways to express
intelligence,
love,
choice,
care,
and concern.

Sean Sprague

We experience this Spirit in our lives as a Spirit of care and generosity.

We experience this Spirit
in our lives
as a Spirit
of truth and goodness,
love and beauty,
care and generosity.

We give thanks
for the men and women
in many places
at many times
throughout human history

who have opened minds and hearts
to the reality of this Spirit in our midst,
searching for words and images
to express human connectedness
with this mystery
and with everything that exists.

We remember
Jesus of Nazareth,
who yearned to set people free
from religious words and images
that bound them
into a sense of fear of this Spirit.

We give thanks for the way
Jesus has led us
to awareness of the Spirit
in our everyday living.
Calling us to be neighbor
in ways that cross religious,
cultural, and social barriers,
he challenges us
to give this Spirit
free reign in our lives
so that the human community
and our own personal lives
may be characterized by
compassion,
genuine care for the disadvantaged,
and concern for justice.

He set us free
so that we would live
"in peace, in God's presence all the days of our lives."

We share this meal,
as Jesus shared a meal
the night before he died.
We take bread,
as Jesus took bread,
and we remember,
as Jesus remembered,
a Spirit of constant presence.

We break
and share this bread,
as Jesus broke and shared bread,
and we give it to one another
as our pledge of openness
to the Spirit of Love in our midst,
and as our remembrance of Jesus
who enlightened our minds and hearts
and who was ready to die for what he believed.

We take this wine
and drink,
as Jesus asked his friends to drink,
mindful of a relationship of love and trust
between ourselves and the Spirit of Life,
ready to allow that Spirit
free expression in all we do.

To being filled with the Spirit of God we say:
Amen.

To having the power of the Spirit at work in us we say:
Amen.

To all that the Spirit can do in each of us we say:
Amen.

To being the body of Christ in our world we say:
Amen.